Betsy Ross lived
from 1752 to 1836.
She may have
sewn the first
American flag.

Have you ever wondered how America
got its first flag? Some people believe
that a woman named Betsy Ross
made it. Read on to learn all about
this famous story.

Betsy had 16 brothers and sisters. There were lots of **chores** to do. Betsy helped with the sewing.

Betsy was born in Pennsylvania in 1752. Pennsylvania was one of the 13 **colonies** ruled by England at that time. America had not yet become a country.

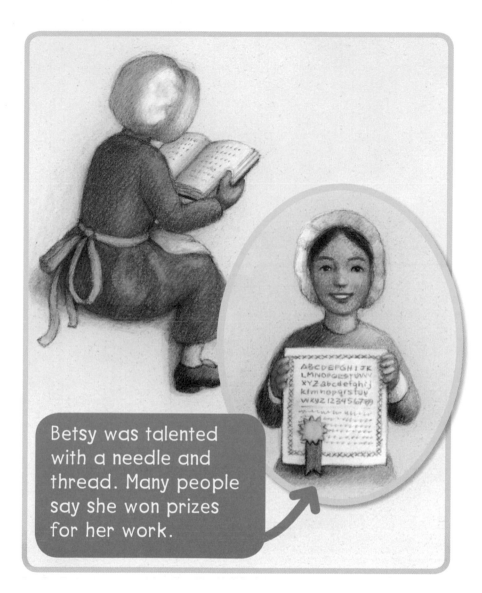

Betsy was talented with a needle and thread. Many people say she won prizes for her work.

Not all children went to school in those days. But Betsy did. She learned to read and write. She also learned how to sew.

Betsy learned to fix curtains, rugs, and even umbrellas. Today, upholsterers mainly make covers for sofas and chairs.

Betsy went to work in an **upholsterer's** shop. There she met John Ross. John and Betsy got married. Later, they opened their own shop.

The colonies formed an army to fight against England. Betsy's husband joined.

But it was a difficult time. A war had started because the colonies did not like England's rules. John joined the army to fight for freedom.

George Washington was not yet president. At that time, he was in charge of the colonies' army.

Betsy decided to run the shop by herself. One day in 1776, General George Washington and two other men met with Betsy at her shop.

George Washington wanted a flag made. It would show that the colonies were free from England. He asked Betsy to sew it.

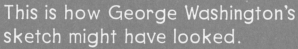
This is how George Washington's sketch might have looked.

George Washington showed Betsy his **sketch** for the flag. It was square. It had 13 stripes and 13 stars. Each star had six points.

Betsy shared her ideas for the flag with George Washington.

But Betsy had different ideas. She said the flag should be a rectangle, not a square. She thought a rectangular shape would fly better in the wind.

Betsy folded the cloth in a special way. Using her scissors, she made a five-pointed star with just one snip!

Betsy also thought the stars should have five points instead of six. She said a five-pointed star was easier to make.

The men made sure that Betsy had money for **supplies**.

The men liked Betsy's ideas. They needed the flag as soon as possible. They asked Betsy to get started on it right away.

1776 Flag

The 13 stars and 13 stripes stood for the 13 colonies.

Betsy worked hard to make the flag. She sewed a rectangle with 13 stripes.

Today's Flag

The 13 stripes stand for the 13 colonies.

The 50 stars stand for the 50 states.

The flag has changed over the years. This is how it looks today.

In one corner, she placed a blue square. In the square, she sewed 13 stars. The stars formed a circle.

No one outside Betsy's family knew her story about the flag.

On June 14, 1777, the design of the first American flag was made **official**. Years later, Betsy loved to tell her grandchildren how she had made the first flag.

You can visit Betsy Ross's house in Philadelphia, Pennsylvania.

In 1870, Betsy's grandson gave a speech. He said that Betsy had made the first flag. No one knows for sure that this is true. But people still like to tell the story of Betsy Ross and her flag.

Glossary

chore (noun) a job that needs to be done regularly, such as washing dishes

colony (noun) land controlled by another country

official (adjective) approved by a group or person in power

sketch (noun) a quick, rough drawing

supplies (noun) materials needed in order to do something

upholsterer (noun) today, a person who puts new fabric on furniture or stuffs it with new materials